Amazon FBA

Fulfillment By Amazon

A step by step Beginners guide to Find, Private label and Sell Physical products on Amazon and make Thousands of Dollars every month.

Table of Content

Introduction

Introduction

I want to thank you and congratulate you for downloading the book, *"**Amazon FBA***: *Fulfillment by Amazon: A step by step beginners guide to find, private label and sell physical products on Amazon and make thousands of Dollars every month. -"*.

This book contains proven steps and strategies on how to start earning as an Amazon seller by using their FBA services. This book is written by me in order to help those people who are trying to explore and start using the FBA program by Amazon.

This book will provide an overview of the selling techniques and procedures by using the Amazon platform. It will guide a seller to position their product in the Amazon market and earn thereby. Through this book, I have shared my experience of learning on how to become a profitable FBA seller.

It will also explain how to increase the earning potential of an individual by harnessing the platform provided by Amazon. By following the step by step guide to sell on Amazon FBA one can easily create their seller account and start sourcing products to sell them at a profitable margin.

This book aims to provide the best guidance while you start your journey as an Amazon seller, right from the scratch. Understand the basic facts and then proceed to source products. Whether you are a big corporation or an individual trying to earn good amount by selling products on Amazon, this book is to help you harness the power of the internet for increasing your earning capacity.

It is not just an attempt to help you understand about Amazon FBA but it is an attempt to guide you through the way when you develop as an FBA seller. It shows you ways for sourcing your products, choosing the right suppliers, ordering your products, sending them to warehouses, promoting your products and finally scaling the business size.

It will be your guide whenever you seek help during your journey of starting as a novice FBA seller to a businessman who will soon be a Platinum seller of amazon!

Thanks again for downloading this book, I hope you enjoy it!

Chapter 1

What is Amazon FBA? - An Introduction

Amazon is one of the largest global online retailers that is a preferred platform for many online marketers and manufacturers for selling their products. Amazon FBA or 'Fulfillment by Amazon' is a business model launched by amazon that allows retailers worldwide to sell their product online by using the customer base and robust distribution network of Amazon.

Amazon with its world class experience in picking, packing and shipping orders helps in boosting the sales of a retailer, whether they are a well-known manufacturer or a startup online trader. It has become one of the most proficient business opportunities and income generating scope for merchants and third party sellers.

Apart from just merchants and online retailers it opens up income generating options for

- People who want to do something of their own,
- Homemakers and stay at home moms,
- Retirees,

- For those who are looking for extra income
- For those who want to sell old stuff

In FBA program Amazon handles warehousing the products, fulfilling the orders from customers and even provides customer service to some extent. It gives an opportunity to the businessperson to act like a corporation, where the hassles are managed by Amazon, and one needs only to concentrate on the procurement of the products they sell.

a. Why choose amazon FBA?

Amazon is an online retailer for more than 20 years now. It has successfully fulfilled millions of orders throughout the world in these long twenty years. Now, with their program 'Fulfillment By Amazon' they are giving an opportunity to the sellers to use Amazon experienced logistic and experience for selling products.

Moreover, when you want to sell your products through your e-commerce store you have to maintain your own warehouse, inventory, and database of your products. Updating them, checking orders, fulfilling them, procuring products in replace of products sold and many more complexities are there. if you choose to use Amazon FBA instead you will be able to use their logistics and warehouse. All you have to do is send your products to their warehouse and the rest will be taken care of them.

While Amazon takes care of your orders you can concentrate on increasing your product line!

Advantages provided by Amazon

Apart from providing you the platform for selling your products, there are various other advantages that you get from an Amazon seller.

- Started in the year 1994, Amazon is one of the most trusted brands for buyers and sellers alike. Being an active seller of FBA program you are able to gain this trust for your business.
- In the US about 44% of household holds an Amazon prime account and when it comes to buying something they prefer Amazon over others. Thus, getting to Amazon FBA program you can leverage this huge customer base.
- As a seller, you can list as many products as you want with Amazon. It allows you to sell products of different kinds and hence you can explore the market at its best. There are no listing fees all you have to pay is a certain amount of membership and a commission over the total sales.
- Even when Amazon sellers use the FBA model they get the opportunity to have

their product in the Buy Box by Amazon, that means you can easily have more views for your product.

Chapter 2

Earning potential

Indeed, Amazon provides a great opportunity to those who want to be independent and earn by utilizing their own skills. The first thing that someone will think before joining this program is how much they can earn? What is the actual earning potential of any businessman by joining Amazon FBA?

Can they earn more by having their e-commerce site or Amazon is a better option?

It is obvious that there is no such structure that will define the earning potential of any seller. However, depending upon the items listed the time when the items are listed and other competitors the profit can be arrived at. For many, it is a4 figure margin while there are many who have arrived at 5 or 6 figure profit margins after doing business on Amazon FBA for few months.

To calculate the exact earning potential you must have an idea about the products that will be sold by you and the Amazon fees that are associated with it. To sell on Amazon you may have to lower the prices but then all these will be done after proper calculation. Thus, you will be able to get the exact figure that can be expected after selling off your products. However, you must also consider the inventory on hand as there will always be some.

Fees associated with Amazon FBA

While calculating the earning potential it is essential to understand the fees that are associated with Amazon FBA. Once you have an idea about them you can decide upon the final prices. The fees are

- Referral fees that are paid by every amazon seller for suing their platform. The standard referral fees are 15% normally, however depending upon the type of product there may be simple variation in the fees.
- Next fees are closing per item fees and it is variable. If any seller is not paying the monthly subscription to Amazon they have to bear this fee above the referral fees. The value of the closing per item is variable and it depends upon the product category.
- The last fees are order fulfillment fees that are an accumulation of three different costs. They are
    - Order handling fees that are charged per order based on the product size tier that the particular product falls into.

- Pick and pack is a per unit fees that is also a standardized cost depending upon the tier of the product.
- Weight handling per pound is charged based on the weight of the product and also the product size tire of the product. This is a variable cost.

To calculate the earnings from a product these fees must be included and then calculations must be made.

Now, still, the question remains that whether to have your own e-commerce site or go with Amazon FBA. If you have confidence that you can earn that goodwill Amazon has you can go with your e-commerce site, till then it is better to reap profits from the brand that is created by Amazon as an online seller.

Chapter 3
Step by Step Guide to become an Amazon FBA seller

It is simple and easy to be an Amazon FBA seller and earn a 5 figure income every month. All that is needed is proper planning so that you are able to do the right things and reach your goal fast. Remember that it is your planning and positive approach towards the goal that will help you be successful and utilize this channel most.

Here is a Step by Step guide to help you plan how can you start your online journey with Amazon and reap the benefits from this world class online e-commerce site.

Chapter 3.1

Creating an Amazon seller account

The first thing to be done for starting selling through Amazon FBA is registering as an Amazon Seller.

For singing up there are different self-service options.

- Go to "sellercentral.amazon.com" and click in the bottom left "selling on Amazon", or
- Go to "services.amazon.com," and then click on either the "Sell on Amazon box" or "Selling on Amazon" link, or
- Go to the Amazon.com homepage and click on "Sell" button at the top

For getting registered you can try out any of the above links. Once you start registering you have to decide upon whether you will sell as an 'individual' or 'professional.'

Individual vs. Professional seller

You can sell at Amazon as either individual seller or professional seller depending upon the goal you are looking forward to.

If you are a college student and doing this for part time income you can join as 'individual' seller, and if you want to make this your income alternative then you may join as 'professional' seller.

Important things to consider before you choose to be an individual or professional seller are

- Monthly fees
  As a professional seller, you have to pay monthly subscription fees of $39.99 for keeping your account active. It does not consider whether you list or sell any product for any particular month.
  For individual sellers, there are no monthly fees applicable.

- Listing fees
  Both individual and professional sellers pay referral fees on the amount of their product sold. Apart from that as an

17

individual seller, you have to pay $0.99/per item unit sold. Professional sellers do not have to bear this as they are already paying monthly subscription fees of $39.99.

As an individual seller, you have to pay $0.99 per unit sold by you and this is charged in addition to the regular Amazon referral fees. That means if you are planning to sell more than 40 units per month you can consider to get registered as a professional seller for saving those extra dollars and get some other benefits.

- Shipping rates
  You can charge any shipping rates from your customer when you are a professional seller on Amazon. As an Individual seller, your shipping rates will be controlled by Amazon.
  Thus, if you want the shipping to be a profit center for you then you must be a Professional seller.
  You must also remember that Amazon charges you their referral fees by combining the product price and the shipping cost. Hence, while considering shipping rates consider this as a factor.

- Listing new products

  As an Individual seller, you have to add only those items in your offerings that already exist in the product listing of Amazon.

  Only Professional sellers can add new items to the listings for offering to buyers. However, there are certain minor exceptions.

- Gated categories

  Amazon, in order to provide their customers with the best experience, has gated certain categories. The products in the gated categories are Clothing, Jewelry/Watches, Shoes, Beauty, and Automotive, Collectibles books, Appliances, sexual wellness, Luggage, Wine and sports collectible.

  Only Professional sellers have the right to apply for selling products in these gated categories.

Hence, after knowing the difference between An Individual Seller and professional seller, you can decide what type of seller you will get registered as.

Registration Process

The registration process in Amazon is very simple and takes less than an hour provided you keep certain information handy while you start registering.

The rules for registering with Amazon vary from one country to another, but here we will discuss the process of registration at Amazon.com in the US marketplace. While completing the registration form you can do that in parts and take your time. The whole process is mentioned here.

- First, you will have to provide your username and password along with your email address.
- Once you sign up you have to provide Amazon information about your Legal business name, contact information, and address. You're business website if you have any.
- You have to provide then with an internationally chargeable credit card along with a valid billing address. It is important as if the credit card is not valid, amazon will cancel your registration.

- Your contact number where you can be reached while the registration process is on. So, keep your phone nearby.
- Information about your Tax identity. It includes your Social security number and Company's federal Tax ID number. While providing information about your Tax identity it will be verified with "1099-K Tax Document Interview." Amazon does so that IRS gets information about any income generated by you from their channel. Tax paying is your responsibility but it is Amazon's duty to report about the revenue collecting sellers of Amazon to IRS.

After completing your registration you will become a seller on Amazon. Now, you will be prompted to list your product and the moment you list your first product your status as the seller will be "Launched" till then you will be a "registered but not launched" seller.

Before you actually list your product you have to complete certain administrative issues. As a new seller, you must have an idea about it.

Selling in Gated categories

As already mentioned earlier there are product categories selling which needs prior permission from Amazon. If you have registered as a Professional seller you must have a certain product line in your mind and when you are selling products from those gated categories you have to seek permission.

Send the un-gating request immediately after getting registered as a Seller on Amazon. This is mainly because you get a 'first 30 days free' offer even as a professional seller. Now, if you are not able to sell your products on Amazon, then what is the use of being an Amazon Seller? You will have enough time to decide whether you want to be a professional Amazon Seller or not!

Sign in to Seller Central and search for the "Products and categories requiring approval." By visiting this link : https://sellercentral.amazon.com/gp/help/help-page.html/ref=ag_200333160_cont_scsearch?ie=UTF8&itemID=200333160

Here, you have to answer various questions asked by Amazon for selling any particular product from any particular category. They may seek for documents, URLs or images to find out if they can give you approval.

Remember that if Amazon asks for images then send images that match the image requirement of Amazon. Be honest while answering the questions and provide required documentation. If you do not get approval the first time, no issues you can try again.

In the meantime, while you are waiting for getting approval on gated categories you can always list the product in those categories that are not gated.

Setting up your Seller Profile

As a new Amazon seller, there are a lot of settings and I recommend that you do it when you get registered. Later you may not be able to change them and face the problem.

To do so click on the homepage http://sellercentral.amazon.com the Amazon portal for sellers.

- **Account Info**

  In this section verify that the information provided by you during registration is correct. If required you can edit the information from "edit" section.

  If you want to change the display name and use some other name than your legal name you can do it so here.

  In Amazon FBA you also need to ensure that you provide accurate "Return Information." this is for those products that are returned by the customers. They may return it to Amazon, but then Amazon will return it back to the address provided by you.

  If you are interested in changing the credit card information you can do so from "Charge Method." While the credit card details are updated your account may be put on hold and it may take up to 24 hours.

- **Notification preference**
Amazon will be sending you a lot of emails on various issues related to your seller account. In this section, you must decide whether a particular email id will be handling all those emails or there will be separate emails handling different types of issues.

Remember that as a new seller you may not get many emails, but once you get busy there will be separate emails for each order and it is quite natural that you overlook some of them and they were important! So, be careful while setting up the notification preference.

- **Return settings**
As mentioned in the case of FBA your returns will be handled by Amazon. In the case of FBA, you have to fill the information about how you want your products returned to be kept with Amazon.

- **Shipping Settings**

  You have the right to choose your own shipping rates. You can set high ones as Amazon FBA seller but remember that keeping the shipping rates too high may affect your ratings and creditability.

- **User Permissions**

  When you have a team working on fulfilling the jobs this is an important setting to be completed. It allows peoples with different emails to view reports and get access to certain Sections of Seller Central. It is best for allowing certain people to get only that information that is required by them to complete their task.

- **Info and Policies**

  You have to describe your business to your customer and hence take few minutes time to complete "About Seller," especially when you are new to customers and they do not know much about you. You can upload your business logo that will be displayed beside the business name.

To let the customers more about your business and products you can add frequently asked questions and so on.

Once completed you are done with registering. Now let's look for the products that will be profitable.

Chapter 3.2
Searching for a profitable niche

Before you start ordering for various products and ship them to Amazon FBA it is necessary that you are sure that they will perform out there. As a newbie, before you jump into doing the business, it is essential that you check out those subtle clues that will guide you to choose a product that can perform on FBA.

This is to help you choose a product niche that will not only start selling once you list them but also help you generate profit down the line.

How Do You Choose A Product To Sell?

While you choose a profitable product niche there are two ways in which you can do that

Path 1 – Choosing a big product niche, or

Path 2 - Choosing a single product that already has high demand.

Path 1 will help you earn handsome money down the line, but as a beginner you can start small.

This is because when you start selling a product of particular niche at the beginning you have to expertise in all the products that fall into the niche. Like if you choose bathroom supplies, you must include towels, towel holders, drawer organizers, sink and shower caddies, fog resistant mirrors, and the list goes on.

As a beginner you have to spend quite an amount of money as well as time to get information about all these different products. Your time and resources will be limited and you have to work hard for selling all of them.

Thus, choosing a single product from any particular product niche is the best route while you are starting off. In the meantime, you can start choosing particular product niche.

Thus, here is the basic list that will help you choose a profitable niche

Area #1 Choose product between the price range $10 to $50

When you choose any product it is always better to choose ones that price ranges between $10 to $50. You have to keep in mind that you are here to make a profit and hence, while you get product list it must have those products that are mainly impulsive buys.

Before buying any expensive item say a refrigerator a consumer will do research but while buying something for $30 they will not do so. Thus, your aim should be to attempt this attitude and sell more and more.

Moreover, while you choose products of low cost your initial investment will be less too.

Area #2 Go for lightweight products

It is always better to choose products that are lightweight to say the maximum weight of 5 pounds. At FBA program the more will be the weight of the product, the costs will go up. With a big size product that is heavy, the shipping cost will be high and your profit will be reduced.

Now, to understand the shipping weight it is important that you know about the total weight of the product. How can you know it until and unless you have the actual product list in your hand?

You can by digging some information from Amazon. Find out what others sellers are listing the weights of their product. Like, you can choose a product that has high demand say men's wallet. If you look for various products listed there you can find that their weights are the bare minimum.

Moreover, a heavyweight product will cost you while you ship that product to FBA warehouses. Moreover, Amazon also charges you for the weight of the product; hence, choosing a lightweight product is a good choice.

Area #3 Products with higher BSR

Amazon provides you BSR or "Best Seller Ranking" for the different products sold by them. If you have a product that has 1000 as BSR and another with 500 as BSR, it is obvious that the demand for the later one is more.

By figuring out the BSR you will be able to understand whether the product will be sold often or not. There are other ways to find out the product that will sell more but then BSR is the best way.

While you view any product details you will find that the BSR in that product category is mentioned there.

Area #4 - Your category doesn't contain any brand names

While you choose any product to make sure that you are not going for any brand. At least as a new FBA seller, you should not try competing with a brand as they have much more skill to market their products.

Instead look for such products that are in common use but do not have only branded products, like a wallet. You'll get wallets that are branded and there is a customer for non-branded good quality wallets too. Hence, do not run after a brand, rather avoid it.

Area #5 - Simple items those are easy to handle

Now, again you have to think about an item that will not get damaged while shipment or will be broken before it is delivered to the doorstep of the customer. Simple items like wallets, chopping boards, yoga mat are a good example.

As you have to deal with less damaged good at your inventory you will find that your profit margin is increasing. So choose products that are durable, does not have any electronic parts, there are no moving parts, and are small and lightweight.

Area #6 - Product can be sourced for 25% or less of the actual sale price

While you sell on FBA you have to remember that you need to manage your profit margin intricately. You must choose items that can be purchased at a low price and sold at higher prices.

This is because you have to keep in mind that there will a number of fees that will be added upon before you finally set the selling price. Hence, to arrive at profit margin you have to calculate all those, like 15% of the cost of referral fees of amazon FBA.

There are online sites to help you calculate the profit margin that can be maintained by you after selling a product and paying all the FBA fees. I have experienced that you must choose items whose sale price will be at least 25% higher than the cost price. The better the gap more will be your revenue.

Area #7 - The product is not a seasonal seller

It is always better to sell those products that are not seasonal. If you can sell a product throughout the year you will be earning revenue the year through. However, for seasonal products, you will have a high demand for any particular product and when they are not in demand you have to pay the warehouse charges.

However, it may not always be possible to choose such product but look for one that is demand for at least 9 to 10 months in a year.

Area #8 - Similar products are being sold on eBay

By now you must have shortlisted few products. Now it's time to find out the demand for the product. Visit a similar site like Amazon, say eBay. Figure the demand for your product on that site.

If there are a number of sellers for that particular product at eBay and amazon it is for sure that you also have high chances of selling your product, even as a new Amazon seller.

Area #9 - Ability to expand your product line down the road

While you start selling on amazon your goal must be to sell more and more online. Hence, it is important that you choose a particular product niche that will be helpful in expanding your business down the line.

Like, you can add those products that your customers are likely to buy along with your product. If you are selling wallets then your customers may also show interest in buying passport holders, credit card holders, and others.

Area #10 - Ability to create recurring purchase opportunities

While choosing the product another thing that is worth considering is whether the product is in recurring in nature. A product that is recurring in nature or the customer may buy associates along with the product will increase your profits.

How? If you can ship more products together the shipping cost of the product will be reduced, thus you can make more profit per sale. Apart from that when a customer returns to your product listing for buying any product again your ratings as a seller will increase.

Area #11- Multiple keywords available for your product

Finally, to make sure that you are selling a product that is easily demanded the product must have multiple keywords. You can know about this in later chapters.

Tools to find good products

Once you know the areas that must be looked after while choosing a product it is now to look for the products. The most helpful tools are

- Alibaba will provide you product listing of overseas suppliers. You can also check out the prices. While you search at Alibaba remember to check the Gold suppliers that will show you results related to the best suppliers around the world.
- eBay is the right place from where you can get more ideas about what products you must sell for. At this point, by visiting eBay you can have an idea about what volume of particular product is in demand at what prices. While you search on eBay remember to search after checking "completed listing" so that you get complete information about the products.
- Amazon, yes it is also the best place to know about the products that have high demand. You can come up with new ideas for researching more about a product with the help of Amazon.

You can also research about the products with the help of Software. There is certain software like Jungle scout, AMZ tracker, Sellers Lab and AMZ shark that helps in reaching your product. You may have to pay something for these services but the results are good enough for the amount you pay.

Chapter 3.3
Looking for suppliers

Now that you know the product that you want to sell through amazon FBA it is high time that you start looking for suppliers. There are suppliers all over the world, in USA, Europe, Asia and other places. Hence, it's not just suppliers that you are looking for, but what you are looking is a supplier who will supply you with quality products at the most competitive prices.

Yes, your aim is not just to look for a supplier. While you choose a supplier you have to focus on few factors.

A supplier can be of different type. They are

- Manufacturer- who actually manufacture the products and sell them to the retailer through their own distribution system.
- Distributors- are the middlemen, also known as wholesalers who buy products from the manufacturers and then sell to the retailers.
- Independent craftsmen- are those people who have the skill of making certain objects of artistry. Generally, they do not deal in bulk.

- Import sources – that are supplier at different countries who collect goods from manufacturers just like wholesalers and imports the good to your place.

In the context of FBA seller it is better that you deal with Import sources; however, you can get in touch with a manufacturer or wholesaler too.

First, make sure that you are dealing with a reputable factory. The supplier should have enough experience and for checking these things you can look for their status in Alibaba or Google reviews can also be helpful. Check out the strength and weakness of the suppliers whom you want to deal with, but before that let's find out how can you source suppliers.

Consider your budget

While you look for suppliers you also have to consider your budget. Until and unless you have enough funds in your hand you should not start looking for suppliers. Now, the question comes how much is enough?

To start with you must have at least $3000 to $4000 in hand. Yes, you must be thinking that is too much, but let's calculate whether it is too much or just fine.

If you buy products worth $2 per piece then for ordering 500 pieces you will require about $1000. After that, you have to consider shipping cost and that will say another $200. You will be spending something around $100 to $200 for photography of the products. You will need certain software for market research and email handling. Hence, all this will round up around $2000, that also for only 500 products at a bare minimum price of $2. So, to start you must have at least $3000 in your hands.

There is no doubt that the more money you can invest, the more results can be expected. However, the goal is to earn maximum profits and grow as an FBA seller and for that, you need to have a supplier who will source your products at the best prices.

Seek help at Alibaba

While looking for suppliers the best place to look is at Alibaba. You will find that most of the sellers head to Alibaba for searching suppliers for their products. Why? Because they are comprehensive, simple, easy and online.

Alibaba provides you with the most comprehensive supplier list on the planet that is complete with catalogs, photos, and information about the products. At Alibaba the Chinese online wholesale market you will find distributors and manufacturers from all over the world. These manufacturers will even work with you so that you are able to create your own brand. At Alibaba, the suppliers are differentiated into various categories like Gold suppliers, Assessed suppliers.

Before you start contacting the suppliers you must know the exact location where the product chosen by you is mainly manufactured. Suppose you are choosing leather belt, then which area is famous for manufacturing of leather belt. Know the details and start looking for suppliers from that area.

As mentioned you will get choices like Gold suppliers, assessed suppliers, and Alibaba trade assurance while choosing suppliers. You must have an idea about these so that you can choose the right supplier.

- Alibaba trade assurance is provided to the buyer (in this case you) as an assurance that if there is any dispute you can submit your claim to Alibaba. If they find that your claim is correct they will help you get your returned. However, your sales agreement with the supplier must contain the points that may create dispute later like lead time, QC etc.,
- Gold suppliers are those factories that are paying Alibaba to show their products favorably. Take it as a good sign as the factory is trying to grow their business.
- Assessed suppliers are those who have a third party visit from Alibaba to check out their facilities.

Hence, if you are not sure of what to look for, you can check out all these three options so you get the best suppliers list in front of you. However, if by chance you have the opportunity to visit China for visiting their factory you may not check at assessed suppliers.

Shortlisting suppliers

After you have checked the supplier's choices you will come up with results. It's time to dig out the gem and for that open suppliers in different pages. Then look for the information related to the points below

Products, Location, Keywords, Time listed as a gold supplier and Time listed on Alibaba.

Look in details about all these. If you find that any particular factory is operating as Gold suppliers for only 1 year, it does not mean that they are operating for only one year. Look for their time as Alibaba listing. They may be operating for 5 or more years before they opt out to become a gold supplier.

Similarly look at the images of the products provided, know about their location. Visit their individual websites and find out if they seem professional there. check out if they provide professional images of tier products or if they mention about their QC process properly. Are the keywords in their pages relevant or they have stuff with irrelevant keywords?

Getting a positive response to these questions will help you shortlist suppliers.

Once you get to hold on some of the suppliers you must approach them to know what are their terms and conditions about doing business with you. Also, ask them whether they will ship the products directly to Amazon FBA warehouses.

Hands on these you must have shortlisted a few suppliers from the huge number of suppliers that you get at Alibaba, that is if you look for "jumping rope" you will find more than 24,000 suppliers!!

After getting a list of suppliers you have to shortlist them and for that proceed with the next step.

A few notes about the Alibaba listings:

- While choosing any company you must not consider a company profile based on the response rate of the company. The RR is the frequency of replies by the supplier by using the Alibaba platform. Now, if the supplier responses directly via email, Alibaba will not count that response!
- Do not try to differentiate between an actual manufacturer and a middleman or sales agent. It is not possible to visit their factory for checking. So, concentrate of the rates that you get for your product and the

trustworthiness and reliability of the supplier.

- If you find that a supplier is asking too much about your company details and background, understand that they want to gauge your potential as a buyer. Before they invest their resources or time for your order they are vetting your buying power. If you feel uncomfortable it is better to look for another potential supplier.

- You must also consider their response rate and the details that are provided by them while responding to your queries. Are they clear about what they want to convey or just providing fake ideas?

Remember to make a pipeline of suppliers so that if you find the samples from the first supplier not up to the mark you can get to the next supplier fast, without spending your valuable time.

Chapter 3.4
Getting samples

Once you did your homework and have chosen the supplier it is the time that you request then for samples. If you are craving to place the order and get it shipped to FBA warehouses, give a halt.

You have seen the images of the product and have not touched the products at all, then how can you be sure of the quality of the products? You have to ensure that the products that you store at the FBA warehouses are good enough to be sold to the customers. If they are not of the good quality you can understand what will happen to your reputation at Amazon. So, work out and request for samples from your supplier.

While your request for samples does not request it to a single supplier. You must have communicated with more than one supplier by now ask from 3 to 4 suppliers. It will help you compare the product and prices and also save time in case you do not like the samples send by the supplier at first chance.

While you place orders to the suppliers for samples make sure that you are providing them with clear instructions. You should be specific about the product samples you want and your communication must be so.

Normally if you are not requesting for a custom sample the supplier should not ask for any price. However, if you are asking them to customize the sample they may charge you for the customization. Also, consider that you have to pay the shipping charges for sending the customized sample. Generally, they must send it by Airmail so that you get the samples fast.

Asking for the sample

The best way to ask for a sample is by sending an email. Now, your email should look professional and must be precise and to the point. You must remember that just the way you are trying to find out the quality of the supplier they too are looking into your credibility and deciding whether they must do business with you.

Structure your email in such way that it professionalism. Your email should be well-organized and have clear questions that can be answered by the reader easily. It should contain details in such way that the receiver understands your requirement clearly by reading the email.

You can ask questions like

- What is the minimum order quantity of the product? Do they take orders in batches of 500 units or more?
- Ask them about the pricing for the samples. Many suppliers do not charge for samples while other provides them at discounted prices. You must ask specifically about it.
- Enquire about the actual production cost per unit. Many times you may get a range

like $2-$4, but you must request to give you the exact rates.

- What is the total production time required for producing your products with customization or without customization?
- Does the supplier need up front payments? What will be the payment terms of the suppliers?

In response to your email, the supplier should also send in specific replies. It's not that they must agree with everything you say. They must explain the cost of samples if anything charged by them, and also let you know about the time that will be required for them to send the samples.

Got the samples? Now?

After you have received the samples it is time to check out the quality. Take out the images send to your earlier by the supplier. Compare the images along with the actual product in your hand. Do they look similar?

Look at the quality of the samples provided. If you have more than one sample from different suppliers you can also compare them so that you know which the best one is. Note the features as it will be helpful while you write the description of your product (you do not have to wait till the products are actually delivered.)

Now it's time to place your order and get the products delivered at the Amazon fulfillment warehouse.

Chapter 3.5
Placing order and sending the shipment to Amazon warehouse

So you have come a long way now. It's time that you place an order to a chosen supplier about whom you find satisfactory responses. As you already have a quotation from the supplier you know the minimum order quantity and the price per unit. Depending upon the production time you are now ready to place your order.

However, you must remember that you should not hurry in placing the order as once placed you have to proceed with the products you get. Order only if you find satisfactory results. If not then you can look out for more suppliers. You must consider the following before you finally place the order

- The samples quality
- Minimum order quantity or MOQ
- Supplier communication and
- Pricing.

Placing the order

Once you have decided about the supplier it's time to place your order. Before you place your final order it is necessary that you negotiate on the price of the product, the minimum order quantity and the production time. You may feel that by negotiating you may not get actual products as the samples.

It is not so, while you negotiate you will be doing so based on the product sample provided to you. So, make sure that before you place the final order you negotiate on the different terms and conditions with your supplier.

While placing the order there are certain formalities that must be maintained by you. They are

1. Have proper documents

While placing orders it is important to have proper documents without which there are high chances that your order may fail. And you too will not have any right to sue the company who has failed your order. So, place your order after fulfilling the various formalities.

So the first step to pace your order is by issuing a Purchase order or PO. It is a commercial document issued by the buyer to the seller that states about the cost per unit of the product, order quantity, has product specification, payment terms, delivery terms and conditions and other relevant information regarding the order. By sending a purchase order to your supplier you are actually sending a legal document to your supplier that states that both the parties have agreed to provide products at mentioned cost.

After the supplier accepts the PO the contract between you and the supplier starts and if they are unable to meet the condition or send different products this document will help you.

Remember that while you make the purchase order you must be specific about certain things. They are

- Description of the products and its specifications
- Total quantity orders and the rate per unit
- Payment terms and how the payment are to be made
- Delivery time and place where delivery will be done
- Different parties to bear the various costs like import duties, shipping etc.

By mentioning all this clearly you are entering into a legal contract with your supplier.

2. Payment terms

You must have decided upon the payment terms earlier but in order to mention it in your PO here are they

- Upfront transfer or bank transfer. If such transfer is done before the supplier starts working on the project it is very risky for you. In the case of an unknown supplier, you should not try this out. Use it later when you have built a relationship with your supplier. You may also use this for providing a certain amount as an advance, but again it is risky for a new supplier.

- Letter of Credit issued by any financial institution. It is a safe procedure for both the parties but the procedure to issue a letter of credit is quite complex. Thus, it is also a preferred method of large consignments.

- Western Union payment is an option that too is risky for the buyer just as bank transfers are. It should be protected by Escrow.

- PayPal is a good option for buyers as the risk here is comparatively less. However, suppliers do not like this as they have to pay taxes while withdrawing money.

- Escrow is the best method where the buyer's money is helping by the third party and it is paid to the supplier only after confirmation from the buyer.

By using any of these methods you can set the payment terms and send your Purchase order and place your order.

3. Sending shipment to Amazon warehouse

When you place the order you must have decided that how can the shipment be delivered to Amazon warehouses. If the supplier does it for you nothing like it, the problem arises when you have to ship the products to Amazon warehouses.

However, if the shipment is directly done by the suppliers to the Amazon warehouses you should be careful about the following

- The supplier must arrange for the customs and import clearance before they deliver the products to the warehouses.

- You must own the Importer of record as amazon will not provide you with the IOR.

- Ensure that the packages have proper labels on them so that they are stored properly.

- Your Tax ID numbers and other documents must be provided to the supplier earlier. Amazon will not provide theirs for any reasons.

- The brokerage or freight forwarding services must be borne either by you or your supplier. Decide upon this while you issue the purchase order.

Different aspects that must be maintained by you before sending in the shipment are

Product labelling

Before you send your products to amazon warehouses it is necessary that they are labeled properly with scan-able barcodes. This allows the fulfillment centers to pick and pack your orders fast while they fulfill your orders.

You can opt to sell your products under Amazon's commingles inventory then there is no need to label your products.

While you label your products be sure of

- That the labels are applied on flat surfaces. Labels that are wrapped at the corners or at curves may not be scan-able.

- If there are other barcodes they must be covered so that multiple visible barcodes do not impede the whole process and result in loss of inventory in future.

- It is best to use laser jet printers for printing the labels so that they are of high quality and does not fade off easily.

- In the label, there must be

  - Title and descriptions

  - Barcode

  - FNSKU that is the Amazon fulfillment center identifier.

  - Product condition.

Next, it is important to put emphasis on the packing and shipment labeling.

Before you label the boxes it is necessary that you consolidate these products into boxes before sending them to fulfillment centers so that you are able to understand them easily.

Amazon has specific rules regarding the product packaging and before you do that it is necessary that you read the terms and conditions.

Make sure that you have read about packaging instructions for the different type of products like loose products, boxed units, sold assets, expiry date items and soon.

There should not be any marketing products like pamphlets with your product. Amazon always puts a stretch on organizing your products separately so that they are able to store your products and ship them fast.

Shipping your products to Amazon warehouses yourself

If your supplier is not shipping the products to Amazon warehouses then you have to arrange for that. You will need to provide amazon the tracking numbers with which they will be able to understand about your products and store them properly.

Remember that every consignment that will be provided by you to amazon must contain the Bill of lading and your carrier should have it. The BOL must include details like Amazon reference number and Shipment ID, the name of the seller, legal name of the seller, Address of seller, carrier name and address, Unit quantity and the type of quantity that is boxes, cartoons etc., and any other markings.

Prior to the delivery, your carrier must have an appointment with fulfillment center and the BOL information must be provided to them. Without it, there may be a delay in the whole process.

Avoid these common mistakes

While doing shipment to amazon Fulfilment centers you must be careful about these common mistakes.

- Beware of mislabelling that is the product does not match with the label on the product.

- There was no label at all when the shipment arrives at amazon warehouses

- The position of the label was such like on any corner or curves that make it impossible to scan and read the bar code.

- Any issues related to shipping of the products.

It is necessary that whether you are shipping the products to the warehouses or your supplier is directly doing that it is your duty to ensure that you read the instructions provided by amazon carefully before you ship your products. Amazon may make necessary changes from time to time, so, before you ship your products it is always better to follow their guidelines.

Steps to do before sending shipment

Before you send your shipment to the fulfillment center here are the simple steps that must be followed.

Step 1. Go to your amazon seller account first.

Step 2. On the home page, you will find settings that lie at the top right corner. Choose "fulfillment by Amazon" that lies at the end of the list.

Step3. You will find outbound and inbound settings there. Edit the inbound settings.

Step 4. Upon entering inbound settings you will get 'Inventory placement services.' From here you can choose to keep all your product shipment at the same fulfillment center. Click on update to ensure that the changes take place.

Step 5. Confirm it as updated and you will get the details of the fulfillment center where you have to send in your shipment.

Chapter 3.6
Listing your products

After completing the procedure of delivering your order at the Amazon fulfillment warehouses it's time to list your products on amazon so that you can start the procedure of selling.

There are different ways in which you can list your product and here I'll discuss the ways that are fit for w new seller like you.

Option #1 — Listing from the Product Page

For a new seller like you, the easiest way to list your product is by finding the matching products at the Amazon site and click on the "sell yours" button.

For searching the matching product you can look for Product Identification number like ISBN (International Standard Book Number), UPC (Universal Product Code), and EAN (European Article Number) or you can simply search by name. Once you get the product make sure that you are listing an identical product.

Now, you have to click on "sell yours" button and then you will be prompted to enter the price, quantity and the condition of the product.

Option #2 — Listing Via Seller Central

This may not be the easiest way to list your product but when you are a pro seller you must list your product via Seller Central.

You can use the 'Add a product' feature in the Seller central when you are listing products by creating them from scratch and listing less than

50 items. It is a simple web-based interface that allows you to list your data individually and not using a spreadsheet for entering the data.

The process of listing your product via Seller Central also depends upon the fact that whether your product is already listed in the Amazon catalog or you are the first one to list such type of product.

Product already listed

If the product is already listed you will have to follow the following steps

- Go to the Inventory Page of Seller central and click on 'Inventory tab.'
- Once you get the drop down menu click on 'Add a product'
- Next is the product ID field where you have to type the UPC code of your product and in case your product is a book or media item enter the ISBN number.
As your product is already listed you can find it in the search result. Once you are sure of the identical products you can start checking the products. After completing the correct listing click on 'Sell Yours' button.
- You will also have to enter the Product SKU or Stock keeping Unit, the condition of the product, quantity and price of each unit. You can add other information too and once you have completed you are ready to 'Save and Finish.' Once you click submit your product is listed on the website for sale!

Product not listed

If your product is not already listed then you have to follow the following steps for listing your products.

- Visit the Inventory page of Seller central and click on the 'inventory tab.'
- On the tab go to the "add a product' and there click on the button 'Create a new product.'
- Now, you have to choose the category of your product. Ensure that you are not listing a gated product without prior permission. You can search the product category by 'Find category' button. You may also search the categories manually by clicking on the link.
- If you are not sure of the category then the best option is to use the search tool. Type in few keywords that match your product and look for the result. Like in our example if your product is men's wallet write it as a keyword. The result page will show the results matching your keyword.
- On the right side of the category result page you will find the possible categories and on the left side of the page, you'll find the high-level categories of similar

products. You can search there to get the specific product category. Like if you are selling 'genuine men's leather wallet' chooses it.

- Now click on 'create a new product' and then select the category and the subcategory of the product. Here you will mention the product attributes that will help your product to be unique from the products that are already listed there. The product attributes are the product name, identifiers, descriptions, and others that are discussed below.

- For your inventory stock keeping purpose, you may add the SKU that will not be displayed on the product page. Apart from that, you have to add descriptions, keywords, and images.

- After entering the required information you are ready to create your listing. If any additional field is required you will find that with an asterisk.

- Finally, you have to select the shipping method. As you are using the Amazon FBA services you will choose Fulfillment by Amazon for shipping the products to your customers.

- Click on 'Save and Finish' to save the data and get your product page ready.

Vital information to be provided while listing

While you list your product you have to notice that you provide proper information under the following headings.

- **Product name**

  The product name that you provide is the title that each customer sees on the listing. It is necessary to put down as many possible keywords in the title. Like instead of mentioning just men's leather wallet, write "Cherry brown genuine leather wallet for men." You can write a product name up to 250 characters, so be descriptive there.

- **Manufacturer and Brand Name**

  If you have your own brand name use that to fill this field.

- **Other details**

  There are other fields that need to be filled by you. They are color, the material used, shape, package quantity, size, Item Display Dimensions and Weight, Weight Supported and others.

- ***Product ID***

  Every product that is sold on amazon has their unique product ID, so your product should also have one. You can seek help from your manufacturers or look at various websites that sell UPC codes in bulk.

- ***Variations***

  It will be the next tab and if you have your product in different variations of colors or size you must mention them here. You'll get a drop-down list with the different types of variations and from that choose one that fits yours. Then fill in the details and go to the next tab.

- ***Offers***

  This is important as you have to select a lot of things here and mention them. Some of them like the Tax code, release date, selling start date will depend on whether you want to fill the details or not. However, as you are using Amazon FBA services you should check the Fulfillment channels stating that you want to take Amazon FBA services.

- ***Images***

  You must upload a high-quality image here that matches with the guidelines provided by Amazon.

- ***Description***

  Product Description is most important as here you can use the related keywords that will be useful for finding your products.

- ***Keywords***

  I'll discuss this in details later in this book.

- ***Other details***

  This is product specific and when you actually start doing it you'll understand whether you will require other details or not.

Chapter 3.7
Optimizing the product for keywords

Whether you call them 'search terms' or keywords, optimization of the important words related to your product is your key to success in amazon FBA. You may have your products stocked at the amazon Fulfillment warehouses and have your listing completed but without proper optimization of the keywords, you may not get results.

To find any product on Amazon a user generally provides search terms for the products. If you can optimize your keywords properly then you can expect good results and you must remember that optimization of amazon search terms is different from that of search engine optimization.

To ensure that your products are listed with a maximum possible combination of keywords you must equip your product with relevant search terms. However, stuffing them may not give proper results so you should do them meticulously. Do not use all of them in the title.

You will find keywords while you complete your listing and there you can put down the keywords or search terms that will be handy while you list your product. You can put those keywords there that are necessary but are not suitable for visible integration like some common misspellings of certain words or colloquial synonyms.

What's Important for Optimization of Amazon Search Terms?

While you fill the keywords you must remember certain rules that will help users recognize all the keywords correctly and you too can use the available space at its best.

There are search terms that are the normal keywords and there are platinum keywords. This is the well-kept secret of amazon that will be used only when you become a platinum Amazon seller. As a regular seller, these platinum keywords will not be taken into account during the algorithm of keywords optimization.

- Fill the search term fields – use all the space
  In the search term, you will find that Amazon has given you 5 fields to be filled with relevant keywords. In each field, you can fill up to 1000 characters that mean you have to all 5000 characters in your hand for writing keywords in the backend. Your aim should be to fill the space with as many possible keywords. In this case, the relative distance from one keyword to another is irrelevant and location too is

irrelevant as amazon treats these five fields as a rational set of keywords.

So you are at the liberty of writing as many relevant keywords you can and not just one keyword for one field.

- Tips on saving space in Amazon's search terms in the back end
As you have a limit of 1000 characters you must aim at saving as much space as possible so that you can utilize the space provided. Just by cutting down a few characters from every keyword will allow you to add many more terms!

Moreover, by using hyphenated words you can avoid repetitions. When two words are connected by hyphen it includes almost all possible combination. Like 'anti-aging' is a keyword that will cover 'anti', 'aging,' 'antiaging,' and 'anti-aging.'

Apart from that, there is no need to distinguish between singular and plural form as they will be included in the search results automatically. In the same way, there is no need to distinguish between lower case letters and upper case letters.

Also, it is necessary that you remove any filler words as they occupy space and do not have any affectivity.

For separating the keywords giving a space between each keyword is good enough. You do not have to insert any comma or any others in. They just use up space.

To illustrate this example of night cream and its related search terms can be taken

These are bad keyword examples

- Night cream,
- Cream for night
- Night, cream, moisturizer, wrinkle remover
- "night cream" "moisturizer" and so on

Instead, the keywords can be

- Night cream moisturizer face wrinkles (to use the maximum characters available)
- Cream night (as a filler 'for' is not required)

- Night cream moisturizer wrinkle remover (use of punctuation is not necessary)
- night cream moisturizer (quotation marks are useless)

Also instead of using platinum keywords at the beginning, it is better to use the 5000 characters for describing the keywords. You must remember that platinum keywords will be of your use only and only when you become a platinum seller.

- Use A Search Term Optimization Tool for increasing visibility

When you are working to increase the visibility of a search term you can try it yourself, but by taking the help of any software you will find that things are becoming smoother and easier. They may cost you certain bucks at the beginning but when you get results from the software you will find it useful.

Benefits of keyword optimization for Amazon

It is necessary that you optimize the keywords for your listings. It not only helps in increasing your visibility but helps in increasing your rank too. Yes, as amazon seller you will have rank and when a customer will order your product they will look at the rank of the supplier in the product category.

It is quite obvious that everybody will like to buy from a buyer who has a good rank when there are others sellers selling the almost same product. You may have better products than your competitors but if your rank does not reflect it, it will be of no use.

Hence, in order to ensure that you have good ranking in the product category, you are dealing you must ensure to have your keywords optimized. They will help users to find your products easily and thus help you increase your sales and upgrading your rank.

Moreover, as you are using amazon FBA program any product listed under this program comes under Amazon Prime. You will also get an 'amazon Prime' mark on your product listing that will let the Prime members know that they can take advantage of their Prime membership. This is indeed an added advantage of taking Fulfillment services by Amazon.

Chapter 3.8
Promoting on Amazon and Facebook

Amazon is a popular e-commerce site where millions of buyers visits and purchases different kind of products. Thus, just by becoming a seller there may not be very fruitful as there are many other sellers who are selling the same kind of items as sold by you.

In order to grow and scale up, it is necessary that you know how you can harness the potential of Amazon and Facebook for promoting your product and increasing your sales. Facebook is the largest growing social network that also helps in increasing your visibility and the demand for your product.

Promoting your product on Amazon

As you have used amazon as the e-commerce platform for selling your product, you have almost done everything for making your visible on a search result. However, the challenge is not to appear on a search result only but to make users search your products instead of searching your product category. Hope you understand the different and for that, you have to harness the scope that is provided by amazon.

There is a program where you can post ads on amazon and other related sites. You have to pay per click on the ads. For some ads, you may have to pay $1 but it really pays back. For another type of ads, you have to bear few cents. When you place ads and users visit your product page you get a better response as the users expect something and they land directly on that page, without looking for other products, Hence, you also face less competition.

Market your products off Amazon site too. To do this you can take help of content. Write blogs for social media and other related sites. You can also post articles on the utility of your products.

Promoting your product on Facebook

Facebook is considered as the largest and the fastest growing social network as it has more than 1.39 billion active users. So, by promoting your product here you have huge opportunity to increase your sales.

Amazon FBA sellers along with leading brands and other e-commerce stores are taking advantage of this platform for promoting their products. By advertising on this platform, they are able to channelize customers towards their products and increase sales.

- What makes Amazon FBA sellers promote their products on Facebook?

Any advertising campaign becomes successful if you know how to target your audience and if the target audience can be separated demographically the whole thing becomes simpler. This is the advantage of marketing with Facebook. It has diversified data from different type of users and with it, a marketer can find out their ideal customers.

Moreover, the whole process of advertising on Facebook is user-friendly, powerful and flexible.

To build up ad campaigns you need not be an expert and you'll get high returns too. Thus, most of the FBA sellers are trying to drive more traffic to their listings by promoting their products on Facebook.

Now, as a new FBA seller, you must be worrying that how can you take advantage of the competitive edge that is provided by Facebook. When you have this book at your disposal you do not have to worry about that. Just keep reading. I have broken up the whole process into simple steps so that you can start doing it all by yourself.

Creating Your Business Page

First, you need to set up your business page. It is a simple process, just follow the steps.

- Select "create a page" from your Facebook account. For this, you may use the drop-down menu from the top right corner of your account.
- Now you have to select a business category. There are different categories allowed by Facebook so that businesses can distinguish themselves easily. Being an amazon FBA seller you can choose "brand or product."
- Now, you have to choose your industry specific category. You need to choose an industry that describes your product best. You also have to provide information about your business. Next, you have to agree to the terms and conditions provided by Facebook. Now click on "get started"
- It's time to launch your page and optimize it. For that
  - Add a suitable and interesting description for your visitors to know about your brand.

- o Upload a nice profile picture that looks professional too.
- o Include a link to your amazon product listing.
- o To check out your page add it to your favorites.

Setting up your Ad Account

The Essential Facebook Ads Types

In Facebook you'll find different types of ads variables, however, here I'll discuss those are applicable for Amazon FBA seller.

- Carousel or Multiproduct ad for showcasing a catalog of product variations to the audience.
- Page boost ads for boosting the visibility of status update of the linked post or Facebook photo update.
- Page post video ads that are auto playing when displayed.

Facebook Ad Creation

For promoting your company by using the Facebook platform you can try out any of the three ways.

- Using the Facebook page and clicking on the page for boosting your existing posts to more and more audience. However, this is not a much-recommended technique.
- Using Facebook Ad Manager that has different features that are user-friendly.
- By using the Facebook Power editor which comes with most advanced features and a great interface.

You can learn about the Power editor once you start using it. it is actually useful for bulk ad creation, split testing, creating different campaigns with the target audience and variable budgets.

How Facebook Ads are structured

When you start using Facebook for promoting your products the first question that you have to reply is what is objective for making the ads so that it can help you optimize your ad. It will serve your ads directly to those users automatically who can perform actions desired by you.

Presently there are 10 options available for objectives but Facebook keep on editing them and you may get more options soon. Some of the objectives mentioned are

- Page likes for increasing the likes on your page
- Clicks on the website so that visitors click on your ads and then visit your website.
- Website conversions for letting the Facebook user reach your web sites particular page.
- Video views to maximize the video views of your ads
- Dynamic product ads that target visitors to your store for promoting your product.

You can select any objective for your ad but you must remember that you still have to pay for every engagement received by your ad. Yes, Facebook optimizes your ads so that you can meet your objective.

You will choose your objective depending upon the objective you have like if you want to increase your fan page views it's better to choose page likes as your objective. In case you want more traffic to your website to choose website conversion as your objective.

As you are an Amazon FBA seller your main goal for Facebook ads is promoting your product and increase sales. There is no such specific tactics or objective that will do this for you, but depending upon your product and your brand identity you can choose an objective. Always keep eyes on what your competitors are doing as you can get an idea about how you should proceed in future.

Selecting Your Audience

It is necessary that you choose your target audience specifically as if they are not specified then there will be no target to which your ads will be campaigns. It will be for all and you'll not get returns as expected. Hence, explore the categories for choosing your target audience.

The options are Location, Age, Behaviors, Relationship, Gender, Education, Work, Politics, Language, Life Events, Interests, and Connections.

You can know more about targeting audience by reading the Facebook manually.

As amazon seller, you already have the contact number of your existing customers. You can use these numbers for retargeting your existing customers and help Facebook in optimizing your customer choices.

Ad Positioning

Sometimes proper positioning of your ad may be very important for getting attention from your customers. Facebook allows you to position your ads in different places and display in various format. It includes mobile ads, sidebar ads, newsfeed and desktop ads.

In this respect, you must also set an Ad budget as if you do not have the budget for your ads you will find that you are losing control over the advertisement cost. You may choose per day budgets or even choose lifetime budgets. There can be a specific start and end dates for your ads or they may run continuously. It is advisable that at the beginning you keep your budget low like $5 to $20 daily. Depending upon the response you can increase the budget gradually.

Facebook Ads Reporting and Analysis

Once your ads are optimized they will be submitted for approval from Facebook and once approved they will be launched automatically. You can monitor the performance of your ad in real time by using the Ads Manager reports. If you do not find response during the first few days do not jump to any conclusion.

You will get various metrics and ones that must be examined regularly are

- Reach of the ad as how many users have seen the ads
- Conversions to check how many users have completed the desired action
- The cost that is paid for getting the desired action.
- The frequency of the ads that is the average number of times the ad is seen by any single user.
- Click through rate will show you the percentage of users who are clicking on your ads.

By comparing these metrics over time you can evaluate your ad response and decide what steps must be taken in order to promote your product through Facebook ads.

Chapter 3.9
Scaling Up

Now it's time to scale up your business. There are a lot of them who started as a small FBA seller and today they are playing in millions. As an Amazon Seller after you has started the business successfully it is the time that you think big and starts scaling your business.

What is it that makes the highly successful sellers successfully? Here, I have pointed out those considerations that will help you scale up your business.

Stay on top of your numbers

In FBA business the main thing that you have to do is source your products and promotes them. Amazon does the rest that is picking, packing and shipping your products. Now, to be a successful seller is not your aim, you need to be very successful so that you keep on growing your business.

For this, you need to keep track on your figures. Selling large volume is not what matters its profit margin that matters the most. Like if you are feeling proud to sold products worth $400000 check out your other figures first. How much of this has been retained by you? What was the operating cost? Are you able to maintain a good margin? Until and unless you keep track on these things you will not be able to accumulate enough to grow your business.

You have to keep checking your overhead costs and when necessary control them. You cannot reduce the fees that you pay to Amazon as FBA seller but what you can do it negotiate with your supplier.

On an average, an FBA seller can make profit of 15% to 20% gross profit over cost. Now amazon platform allows them to make huge sales that make it possible for them to grow. Hence, it is required that you maintain the margin and ensure that you are able to gain that much from your products.

If any of the products sells at a lesser price or is not able to provide you the required return, think of increasing the price. If it is not possible, shift to another product. Remember, to scale up you need to plan from the beginning and keep your numbers ready.

Inventory Management

For scaling up your Amazon business inventory management is another tool that needs your attention, right from the beginning. What is the condition of your stock in hand? Are you losing your sales figures due to your closing stock? If you have inventory at the warehouse you have to bear the storage fees and that too can be a huge amount of your operating cost.

As you expand your business you will be handling a huge number of products and it is then managing your inventory becomes more important.

There are different ratios that will be helpful in deciding whether your inventory is maintained at the right amount or not. Some of them are Inventory to sales ratio, Total inventory value lying with you, the age of inventory, unsold inventory, and others.

To manage your inventory it is necessary that you get some software that will help you know what the condition of stock in your hand is. With the help of a good software, you can know when it is time order any product, which products need to be circulated more, as they are accumulated for long in the warehouse and many more things. Before you scale up you should make the foundation strong and among that inventory management is most important.

Build a Website

When you had started selling on Amazon you didn't have any website, but with the help of a website you can boost your web presence and create a brand of your own. Your website is your own platform apart from the one provided by Amazon, where you can say about yourself, your business ideas and ideology.

There is no doubt that amazon is a great platform to work with, but it will not propagate your thoughts as it has million other sellers like you. So, for that, you have your own website. It will also help you reach your targeted customers fast and email them about your plans.

Moreover, many buyers before buying from you will like to visit your website to know about you and your business, (remember you did the same with suppliers?) if they do not find any website of your own they may lose faith in you and your business may not grow.

If you have your own website you can market your products from there too as there you will not have any competition, you are the only seller there! so, this is another pillar that must be constructed before you start scaling up your business.

Do Something You Enjoy

To grow your business you need to be motivated as until and unless you are passionate about it, you won't be able to grow. You are at the last chapter of the book and that shows you are passionate about your business so, in order to grow your business think of ideas doing which is enjoyed by you.

Selling may motivate you in the beginning but do the same thing for years to come may not. Hence, do that what you enjoy most, I'm not telling you to leave your business but you should deal in products that help you think big!

Do not miss out building relationship with your suppliers. In the long run, they will be of great help.

Improve Your Best Seller Ranking

To grow your business at amazon you need to improve your Bestseller ranking. Most of the time when the same product is sold by different sellers, a customer decides to buy from that seller who has better ranks. So, you must also concentrate on your rank. You have to outsell your competitors, and that easy to say but hard to achieve. Of course, although it's hard to achieve it is not impossible!

There are different ways in which you can, like

- Incorporate proper keywords and optimize them
- Try to figure out how can you increase your hourly sales
- Try to get more and more reviews of your products, it helps in getting better ranks.
- Concentrate on your product description and have an enticing photograph of your products. It is them that make your customers buy products from you.

Even after trying all this you can find that your sales are increasing but your rank is not then you need to think of some other category. Anyways, work hard and you'll surely get results fast. If you find it challenging them to shift your focus to a less competitive category. You must aim to have a higher seller ranking.

Find a Competitive Advantage

What is it that will make customer buy products from you? You'll find that the most successful sellers have some competitive advantage over others that makes them so successful, like someone selling kitchenware has the best chef in the country cooking with their products!

So, you too must aim at such marketing plans that will give you the best results and of course a competitive advantage over others. it is something that cannot be gained within few days. You have to build up relationships and over the years of your business, you'll find you have some.

Like you can build a good relationship with your suppliers and after time they provide you better rates than they give to other competitors. Your competitors can replicate almost everything that you do, but building relationship is something that is unique to you and only you can manage it!

Have Good Systems in Place

Finally, in order to grow, you should have a good system operating for you. You cannot think of growing all of your own. You will need help from an efficient team for providing you support while you grow.

It's true that you must be thinking that when you have FBA to fulfill your orders what is the use of hiring more people and taking the pain of managing them? Is it only picking, packing and shipping your products that matter? Can you manage everything else?

By this time you must have the idea about the other things that you have to manage for growing your business apart from fulfilling your orders. Yes, you will need helping hand to keep your figures traceable, for marketing your products, for looking new products and so on.

There is software that will help you do all this but with a team, you can manage things better. Whether it is accounting or inventory management you can seek help from different software. There is even software that will help you buy 'buy box' of Amazon by re-pricing your products. Setting up your business from the beginning is the key to successful scaling up, not only as FBA seller but also in your business.

Conclusion

This book is an attempt to explain the basics steps that will help a novice online businessman to start up their amazon business. it puts emphasis on Amazon FBA as there the businessman has to concentrate on the core business and the shipment and customer acre will be taken acre by Amazon.

This is a step by step guide to help you understand each steps string from opening your Seller account to scaling up your business. It has covered every aspect of your business.

The methods used are mainly those that are commonly used by any FBA seller. If you want you can try out other references for getting suppliers or shipping your products to amazon warehouses.

Amazon is the most widely used e-commerce site of this world and by starting your own business you can grow big.

Thank you again for downloading this book!

I hope this book was able to help you to start your amazon FBA business.

Finally, if you enjoyed this book, then I'd like to ask you for a favor, would you be kind enough to leave a review for this book on Amazon? It'd be greatly appreciated!

Thank you and good luck!

www.ingramcontent.com/pod-product-compliance
Lightning Source LLC
Chambersburg PA
CBHW070718210526
45170CB00021B/587